The Five-Minute Renaissance
How to have a fuller, richer, happier life in just five minutes a day...really.

Copyright © 2010 J.M. McKee

iUniverse books may be ordered through booksellers or by contacting:

iUniverse
1663 Liberty Drive
Bloomington, IN 47403
www.iuniverse.com
1-800-Authors (1-800-288-4677)

ISBN: 978-1-4502-0499-6 (pbk)
ISBN: 978-1-4502-0498-9 (ebk)

Printed in the United States of America

iUniverse rev. date: 1/21/2010

The FIVE-MINUTE RENAISSANCE

*How to have a fuller, richer, happier life
in just five minutes a day...really.*

J.M. McKee

iUniverse, Inc.
New York   Bloomington

For

Imogene and Ella

Contents

The only joy in the world is to begin.

Cesare Pavese

Nothing is worth more than this day.

Goethe

Introduction:
The Discovery

I'VE READ MY SHARE OF self-help books. All promise happiness and success if you'll just do this or think that. They did help. I'd do this or think that and feel better for about, well, five minutes.

Very little stuck and I felt more frustrated than before. I could now tack on a lack of stick-to-itiveness to my many flaws. Sometimes, while thumbing through books in the self-help section, I'd have the urge to do something, anything except stand there reading self-help books. I would flounce out of the store and actually begin to feel better as I walked. This reinforced the funny feeling I often had in that particular aisle of the bookstore, a feeling that seemed to urge me to stop reading, stop thinking so much, stop looking for an answer and start doing. Action always made me feel better and it was, of course, the only thing that worked.

Anyway, life went on, I did lots of doing and I never went down the self-help aisle again. Yet, there were still things I wanted to do. I had a million excuses; some even made sense, like a lack of time. A few took on an aura of fearfulness. I was genuinely afraid to do some activities. I had a myriad of reasons for this fear. I possessed the ever-popular fear of failure, dreaded the idea that someone might laugh at my endeavor, and saddest of all, didn't think I deserved even to try the thing I most wanted to do. The craziest reason probably was feeling like my wants didn't matter. My wanting to do something might take away from the needs of my spouse, my friends, my work, my children. Through painful experience I learned that forsaking one's needs for another's never works. Life goes out of balance. Just as the inverse is true, ignoring the needs of another eventually produces an out-of-balance relationship. Then of course there were things I knew I should do– pay those bills! clean out that refrigerator! –but sticking needles in my eyes sounded like more fun.

Then my kids turned into teenagers. They didn't want to do anything I wanted them to do. Practicing piano, exercising, reading and cleaning their room all fell to the wayside for want of time and/or inclination.

It was the trials at the piano that led to my discovery. No one in my household is going to play Carnegie Hall so practicing to get there, as the old joke goes, was totally unnecessary. Still, I believed there was great value in learning to play an instrument and I wanted my children to have that experience. I spoke to music teachers and professional musicians and asked all of them about practicing. The musicians were unanimous; someone had encouraged them to practice. Well, I was encouraging my kids and it wasn't working. The teachers all said, "One half hour a day, minimum." No way were my kids going to practice for a half hour a day. Finally, a friend who teaches the fiddle said, "You can practice five minutes or five hours". He meant, of course, practicing is up to the individual. Again, my kids were not going to practice five hours, but it occurred to me that five minutes was doable even in the busiest of lives.

So I set up the five-minute rule. Just five minutes a day. No more. The secret here is that everyone has five minutes a day. I even joined them and began, a rank beginner, tapping away at the piano for five minutes a day. We all instantly went from never practicing to practicing five minutes a day. From week to week the teacher noticed the improvement in our playing. My kids were happier. They saw that even a tiny bit of doing produced a result. Occasionally, the five minutes would spill over to a few more as the simple act of doing produced positive feelings. Hey, I was on to something here. Maybe I could expand this rule to encompass cleaning and exercising.

In the coming months I did just that, expanding the rule and finding life becoming more fun. I felt more confidant and in control of my life than ever before. I wanted to help others feel this way. I even used the five-minute rule to write this book. It is my heartfelt desire that you find the rule as revolutionary as I have. Certainly it is worth a try. After all, it is only five minutes....

*You don't have to see the whole
staircase, just take the first step.*

Martin Luther King, Jr.

In our leisure we reveal what kind of people we are.

Ovid

Part One:

GETTING STARTED—OR
THE RENAISSANCE BEGINS

Whatever you can do or dream you can, begin it.
Boldness has genius, power, and magic in it.

Goethe

Less is more.

Robert Browning

Why the Five-Minute Rule Works

"IF YOU NEED SOMETHING DONE, give it to a busy person". There is just something about having only a finite amount of time that concentrates the mind. Concentration is, of course, the underpinning of efficient work (or play).

A sense of mastery or accomplishment is an incredibly pleasurable feeling. Maybe you are one of those people at weddings who get up and participate in line dances. If not, you have surely taken in such scenes. People are smiling and obviously having a wonderful time. Knowing simple steps in a dance gives a person a sense of mastery. This particular feeling of mastery is essential to happiness. These are feelings we can have daily. The job promotions, windfalls, milestones and other happy and exciting events are exhilarating but fleeting. The sense of mastery we can have with just five minutes of doing is something we can obtain every day.

Because we are only spending five minutes on an activity, it pretty much limits us to something doable. For example, say you are studying Spanish for an upcoming trip. With only five minutes a day scheduled, you are limited in the amount of difficulty you can take on. Limiting the amount of difficulty provides the opportunity to reach the "sweet spot"– that moment when one successfully meets a challenge. If you had half an hour, you might expect to memorize a few phrases. You would certainly have time to read over many. You may wonder which to pick. What are the most important phrases to know? A half hour later you could very well still be deciding what to study first. With only five minutes, you pick two phrases that appeal to you; learn them and you are done. These phrases may roll around in your head until the next day. Very likely they will remain in your memory, and during the next day's five minutes you will add two more phrases. The feeling of accomplishment will be strong and sweet. You will look forward to continuing the next day.

It may seem as though I am advocating that you should expect very little of yourself so as not to be disappointed. But there is another way of looking at the five-minute rule. Expect to accomplish something, however small. Expect something concrete, something you can take away after the five minutes and say, "I did that." If you spend too much time at the beginning of a project it is easy to feel like the reward of accomplishment and mastery does not equal the time put in.

The five-minute rule also works by taking away the intimidation factor. First, you are limiting the difficulty so you can almost be assured you will meet with success. Second, you must limit your choices of what to do because; after all, you only have five minutes. Take, for example, the old advice: do one thing a day for your career (or social life or whatever). This is too vague, too many choices, too scary. With five minutes you HAVE to do something. You have to fill exactly five minutes with your activity. You must choose something. Even if you are fearful, it is only five minutes.

Finally, the five-minute rule relieves you of the "I'm too tired," excuse. We have all had the experience of feeling spent after a long day of work. Then, by chance we run into an old friend, have a brief conversation and continue on with more energy than we had moments before. The five-minutes you spend on your chosen activity, even when you are tired often has a similar effect. Those few minutes of concentration on something you want to do invigorate the mind.

A single day is enough to make us a little larger.

Paul Klee

Things won are done; joy's soul lies in the doing.

William Shakespeare

Cool Stuff that Happens

You never have a day that feels "wasted". Even the worst I'm-spinning-my-wheels days are redeemed by just five minutes of doing.

Even cooler is that weekends, holidays and vacations no longer "fly by". Having "done" your five minutes, the rest of the day seems full of possibilities. Just spend that little bit of time on something you truly want to do and suddenly your day is about living. The feeling of accomplishment from those five minutes makes your day fuller and more enjoyable. Your day is about doing and it feels wide open. The more you do the bigger your life becomes.

It gets even cooler. You will find yourself looking forward to your five minutes not only because you like the doing and the results. You will also discover that you will look forward to feelings of accomplishment that will pervade your entire life. Doing more without stressing over it is now within your grasp. You trust yourself as a person who "gets things done". Your confidence grows.

That elusive holy grail of "inner peace" is really peace of mind. Peace of mind is achieved when we know we have done our best. We feel in control of our life. It only takes five minutes!

Faith in oneself is the best and safest course.

Michelangelo

Pleasure in the job puts perfection in the work.

Aristotle

Choosing an Activity

MAKE A LIST. JUST START writing. No one will ever see this list. Be bold, silly, outrageous and honest. Let every inhibition fall away. List everything from the most mundane things you want to get done to the things you dream about doing. Now, choose only one. Don't second-guess. Listen to your heart, your gut. Pick the one you REALLY want to do.

Choose the one activity that jumps out from your list, the one you really want to do. Right now, take five minutes and do it. Even if you don't have the supplies or it must wait until a weekday or whatever, you can still start. Do some research. Make a phone call. Begin.

Want to plant a garden? Get out there and till the soil, with a spoon if that is all you have. Have you always wanted to paint? Find those watercolors. Want to read more? Grab that book. Study a subject? Go online and start your research. Exercise? Any doctor will tell you five minutes a day is better than none.

Your activity may be goal directed. That longed for trip to Paris would certainly be enriched by a rudimentary knowledge of the language. How about five minutes a day of free online French lessons? An activity might be something for stress reduction, say meditation or visualization. Whatever your activity, it is likely that you will find, those five minutes will actually relieve at least some of your stress. Stress is largely a feeling of being helpless or out of control. Those five minutes will leave you feeling more in control of your life and the accomplishment from those few minutes will be proof that you are not helpless.

A word about spending money on your activity: many activities can be done with little or no expense. I strongly recommend choosing something that will cost you very little as your first activity. As you move along with the five-minute renaissance, you can be creative if what you really want to do is somewhat expensive. Want to play the piano? Renting one might be an option.

A journey of a thousand miles begins with one step.

Lao-Tzu

*All life is an experiment. The more
experiments you make the better.*

Ralph Waldo Emerson

How to Do It

WELL, YOU JUST GO AHEAD and do your chosen activity–
for five minutes a day. It really is that simple.

You may find it helpful to do your activity at the
same time each day but this is entirely up to you. Above
all, don't judge yourself and don't let anyone judge you.
If possible, don't even let anyone know what you are up
to. This is for you.

As you begin your five-minute activity let yourself
relax into it. Concentrate fully. If you are tired, remind
yourself that you can rest in five short minutes. If you are
worried, know that in five minutes you can restart your
worries. Should you be tremendously busy, be aware that
you can get right back to your duties in a few moments. In
other words, whatever may be going on in your head, you
have only five minutes to focus on something you enjoy.
Your complete immersion in those few moments can have
a remarkable impact on the rest of your day.

Who reflects too much will accomplish little.

Johann Friedrich von Schiller

Inaction saps the vigor of the mind.

Leonardo Da Vinci

Putting the Rule into Practice

A FULL FIVE MINUTES, TIME yourself. And only five minutes, at least at first. And it has to be every day. If it is something you can only do, say, at work, well then every day you are at work. But you have to do it every day that is permissible and available. The rule is five minutes a day, very important. Both the duration and the day in day out quality are vital. The positive feelings you experience from the doing plus the knowledge that you do it everyday and for only five minutes are key. Your days of doing begin to pile up and your sense of accomplishment will grow accordingly.

Knowing you will keep doing the activity for five minutes every day in the future will build your confidence about your capabilities. Soon you may want to add another five-minute activity. This is definitely possible, but for now do only one. Let that become part of your day. If you have picked a winner, you will look forward to your five minutes. It will become more than a habit. It will become a welcomed part of your life.

The secret of getting things done is to act.
Dante

A wise man will make more opportunities than he finds.

Sir Francis Bacon

Part Two:

EXPANDING THE RENAISSANCE

You can't try to do things, you simply must do things.

Ray Bradbury

Far and a way, the best prize life offers is the
chance to work hard at work worth doing.

Theodore Roosevelt

Adding More Activities

ADDING AN ADDITIONAL ACTIVITY, IF it occurs at all, probably should not happen for at least six to eight weeks after starting your first activity. It may be months or years before you want to add another activity. Eventually having two or three five-minute activities may be just right for you. On the other hand, you may be a one activity a day person like me. I switch my activity after a goal is met. I would like to do more than one activity but right now just one fits into my life. Sometimes an activity grows from its original five minutes to be much more. It may become simply a good habit or a new hobby. It could even morph into a new line of work.

Sometimes there is something you have always wanted to do but just never found the time or the initiative. The five-minute rule works well when you need to "break into", something new. Say you have always wanted to go back to college or take a specific class. Take five minutes to look online at the places to study in your area. Make note of some phone numbers and web sites. The next day make a five-minute phone call to ask about tours or having literature sent to you. The next time you are near the college or school take a detour and walk around for five minutes.

Separating these activities into five-minute chunks will pave the way to getting what you want. Each activity is small enough not to intimidate and big enough to let you become comfortable with this new endeavor. This familiarity will most likely give you a feeling that what you want is not so outlandish. In fact, it is probably something well within your abilities. There will be setbacks. There always are. But dealing with them in five-minute chunks makes them surmountable. Surmounting obstacles is tremendously satisfying.

You owe it to us all to get on with what you are good at.

W.H. Auden

You just keep pushing. I made every mistake that could be made. But I just kept pushing.

Rene Descartes

Adding More Minutes

IF YOUR FIVE-MINUTE ACTIVITY IS going to evolve into a much larger part of your day, you will know this relatively quickly. Naturally, over time the positive feeling you get as you do your five minutes will propel you into a few more minutes and quite possibly even a few more minutes. Work as long as you like and no more. Some things will remain at five minutes; some may go to five hours. The five-minute rule lets you discover this. But always remember that only five minutes is ever required.

I have a friend who uses the five-minute rule for exercising. Most days he takes an early morning walk. There is a playground on his route and he always stops to do five minutes of calisthenics. He tells me he has been tempted to do more minutes but always stops at five. He explained that doing more could turn the exercise into a chore. Listening to your feelings is so important here. Trust yourself and know that whatever happens, five minutes is all that is necessary.

Inevitably, frustrations crop up, or fatigue sets in, fear creeps back, setbacks occur or life simply intervenes. Knowing that you can always go back to just five minutes a day will make it less likely that you will stop altogether. Getting to that first minute can be hard in times of fear or adversity but the other four can propel you through the stressful times. But be assured, five minutes a day is all that is required. Anything more is icing on the cake.

The ordinary acts we practice every day at home are of more importance to the soul than their simplicity might suggest.

Thomas More

What can be done at anytime will be done at no time.

Scottish Proverb

Taking on Short–Term Activities A.K.A.–Activities You Dread but Have to Do Anyway

PROCRASTINATION. "NATION", IS QUITE RIGHT. Everyone does it at least a little. It makes us feel, at best uneasy, and at the other end of the spectrum, out of control.

The five-minute rule is the perfect antidote to procrastination. Avoiding that stack of mail? Put in just five minutes. It's probably enough time to open the envelopes, take in the news, throw away all of the junk and place the actual papers of importance in a pile. Not so bad, right? Tomorrow another five minutes and voila a bill paid and one paper filed. How do you feel? I know I feel a little more in control of my life and a little less intimidated by the chore.

Some duties are just plain boring. Cleaning the bathroom, picking up the clothes thrown over the chair and washing the dishes are just a few of the things that we tend to put off. Plan on taking just five minutes to tackle one task. Set a timer. The amount you accomplish will be a happy surprise.

Then there are the tasks we actually want to do, but we are afraid. These are the hardest tasks because we feel-usually erroneously-we are not up to them. But the five-minute rule can always get you started, and sometimes that is all it takes. Whatever gives you that sinking feeling–

asking someone out on a date, looking for a new job, organizing your tax documents–give it just five minutes. Often a phone call will launch your endeavor. Maybe you need to do some research. Put in five minutes today and regardless of the outcome, put in five minutes tomorrow. The fearful feelings may be there, but knowing it is only for five minutes makes the task doable. Much more often than not, you may be astonished by your feelings after your five minutes. "Hey, that wasn't so bad!"

The only cure for grief is action.

George Henry Lewes

Do not dwell in the past, do not dream of the future,
concentrate the mind on the present moment.

Buddha

Using the Rule as a Distraction from Unpleasant Habits or Moods

Smoking, compulsive shopping or eating, biting your nails, whatever your bad habit, you can break it for five minutes, right?

Heading toward the fridge because you're bored, lonely, tired, unhappy, frustrated? This is the perfect time for your five-minute activity, or even a short-term activity. Because it is only five minutes, you will most likely be able to intercept yourself before you make it to the kitchen. After all, you can still head for the goodies post activity. However, those five minutes will give your mind a break from the emotion. You will feel a sense of accomplishment. You may skip the kitchen altogether or if you do make the trip, your choices will reflect a quieter, healthier mindset.

Feeling down in the dumps? Everyone does from time to time. We wouldn't be human if we didn't. Sometimes we have good reason and other times we struggle to find a cause. Either way, a little activity can go a long way in bringing us back to our happier, more productive selves.

You can't wait for inspiration—you have to go after it with a club.

Jack London

Well begun is half done.

Aristotle

Using the Rule to Overcome Inertia

THE FIVE-MINUTE RULE IS PERFECT for when you know you need to spend more than five minutes but you just can't get started. Exercise and writing are often at the top of many people's lists in this category. You are not going to exercise for just five minutes, though. Well, why not? Of course you can work out for five minutes. Once you get moving you will likely stay with it for a few more minutes. If not, stop after five minutes. Those are still well spent minutes. You had a small workout, you listened to your body, and you kept a commitment to yourself. This day, for whatever reason was just not your day to exercise. Tomorrow is another day, and you will put in your five minutes, and possibly more, once again.

Fortunately, there is one form of exercise that only takes five minutes and many people have found it to be a miracle. I am referring to specific medically approved exercises for back pain and the five-minute rule works perfectly. Weak muscles and a lack of flexibility often cause back pain. Some people are incredulous when their doctor gives them an instruction sheet for back exercises rather than a prescription or a recommendation for surgery. When you are in so much pain, it is hard to imagine that simple, regular exercise could fix the problem. Yet, for many sufferers who decide to adopt a steady program of medically approved exercises, the results are beyond their imagining. Forty years ago, after repeatedly throwing her back out and enduring terrible pain, my mother went to her doctor and came home with an exercise instruction sheet. After several weeks, the results were so astounding she continued the regimen. Every morning before she gets out of bed she begins her routine, which she finishes on the floor. She has been pain free for all of these forty years. Possibly, my mother is the first "Five-Minute Renaissance" woman.

Sometimes it is fear that keeps us in a rut. I had always wanted to ballroom dance. No one I knew wanted to take a class with me so I put it off. I was too intimidated to go by myself. One day, I was passing by a ballroom dance studio and I said to myself "I will just go up and grab a flyer". It took a few minutes for me to pick up the schedule and take a quick look around the studio. My five-minute visit calmed my fears. I took a class and was hooked!

The desire to write is strong in many people. Writing is an effective way to sort out thoughts and give weight to feelings, events and ideas. Writing forces us to analyze facts and grapple with complicated concepts. Our thought processes become more effective with writing. I know I am not alone in achieving a feeling of calm when I write.

Yet despite the many benefits of writing and a real desire to begin, we often push it aside. Even composing letters or emails to friends or blogging about a subject you are interested in can seem too much. Writing that novel can be intimidating. Researching for a non-fiction book on your area of expertise can seem time consuming. Keeping a journal may seem like an indulgence, but the act of writing and having your thoughts on paper is satisfying indeed. It does not matter whether it is for you or for others to read.

Now, sit down with pencil and paper or bring up a blank document on your computer. Write for five minutes. Set the timer. See what happens.

*What a wonderful life I've had! I only
wish I'd realized it sooner.*

Collette

*Indolence is a delightful but distressing state;
we must be doing something to be happy.*

Mahatma Gandhi

Stop Wasting Time and Learn to Love the Renaissance Life

THERE ARE DAYS, OR EVEN certain times of nearly every day, that you find yourself wasting precious time…and all time is precious. Occasionally, wasting time can be productive. We recharge our batteries while we do a whole lot of nothing. Unstructured time allows for daydreaming. We can let our minds wander and give our bodies time to relax.

This, of course, can get out of hand. There can be too much of a good thing, and we find ourselves wasting our own precious time. Frustration creeps up. We might try a few distractions such as eating or looking at some sort of screen. But in the end, we know this is just not how we want to spend the minutes of our lives.

A quick glance at a clock and you can be on to five minutes of productivity. Pick anything! Just about any activity will be better than wasting your own time or distracting yourself with mindless endeavors. Maybe you will read for five minutes or make a couple of thirty-second drawings of your cat. How about doing those dishes quickly? Straightening that shelf or doing some push-ups might be satisfying. Anything at all that you can do immediately and will make you feel good is perfect. Hug someone, call someone, brush the dog, clean out the tub, make a to-do list, or listen to music. The list is long with your true desires.

Having utilized your time, or rather, lived your life more fully, you will once again have that wonderful feeling of accomplishment. It takes awhile but that feeling becomes addictive. It is a habit you will love having.

Victory belongs to the most persevering.

Napoleon Bonaparte

If not now, when?

Rabbi Hillel

Part Three:

KEEPING THE
RENAISSANCE ALIVE

Energy and persistence conquer all things.

Benjamin Franklin

*Success is to be measured not so much by
the position one has reached in life as by
the obstacles which he has overcome.*

Booker T. Washington

Falling Off the Wagon—
or Never Say Retreat

First, why do we fall? We might miss a day or two when we are too sick to do much of anything. It is very important to rest but equally important to jump back on as soon as we are able. Good feelings enhance healing.

A lack of time, occasionally, can be a reason. There are days that are so packed a person may not sit down all day. But most days have five minutes somewhere and they are just for you.

More likely the problem is fear. It is perfectly normal. Fear is necessary for our protection but it can bubble up around things we want, simply because they are unfamiliar. Here is where the five-minute rule shines. It's only five minutes, so it's not too scary and the satisfaction we get feels so good it trumps the fear.

When a day goes by and you haven't done your five minutes, you may feel nothing, or feel like verbally beating yourself up. Either of these reactions should be taken seriously. It is possible the activity is not what you really want. No problem. Just go back to your list, add to it, delete from it. This is your list, be unfettered, free, honest, and without judgment. Then put it away for at least an hour. When you go back to it, pick whatever you want. First thought, right thought. Trust yourself.

Now on the other hand, if you miss your activity,

miss the sweet spot where challenge and ability meet, then you know you've picked a winner. Jump back into your activity and enjoy the ride. It will take you somewhere, possibly somewhere totally unexpected and surprising. I will be very bold and amend the saying "Do what you love, the money will follow" to "Do what you love, the rewards will follow." Money could be one of your rewards, but it certainly doesn't have to be the only one.

A word about being hard on yourself when a day goes by and you don't get in your now satisfying five minutes. Honey, it is so easy to fall off. Everyone does it. Getting back on is not difficult, but yes, you do have to jump and you have to jump quickly. Jump right back on cause the wagon just keeps rolling. The wagon of course is your life.

*You cannot teach a man anything; you can
only help him find it within himself.*

Galileo

The great aim of education is not knowledge, but action.

Herbert Spencer

Renaissance Kids

FOR SOME REASON, YOUNG CHILDREN seem to have a natural suspicion about any activity done for just five minutes. It seems like an impossibly short time and how in the world could anything be accomplished in five tiny minutes. So be specific. Set a timer. Have the child sit at the piano or stand in front of their messy room. Then have them perform only until the timer rings. They will be pleasantly surprised by their accomplishment even if they don't admit to it. And they probably won't.

Older children and teenagers will benefit the most by seeing the five-minute rule in action. But since the Five-Minute Renaissance works best when done privately and without fanfare, leaving this book where they might pick it up would be a great start. This may start a conversation. Teens, especially, are often loath to do things that their parents are doing. But the seed will be planted. It may take years but they will know they have this tool. Until then, leave *The Five-Minute Renaissance* lying around for their perusal.

Self-development is a higher duty then self-sacrifice.

Elizabeth Cady Stanton

One's real life is often the life one does not lead.

Oscar Wilde

Possibilities

Reconnect with old friends
Make new ones
Spend time listening to your kids or companion
Start that craft or hobby
Learn a new language
Become an expert on a subject
Learn to play an instrument
Meditate
Become efficient on a new computer program
Keep a journal of things for which you are
    grateful
Explore a new line of work
Communicate with your loved ones through
    letters or emails
Show your loved ones affection
Explore volunteer activities
Exercise
Learn how to play chess
Learn some dance moves
Clean out those closets
Write
Paint
Straighten up your living space
Listen to music you love or discover music that
    is new to you
Read the classics
Find recipes for delicious food
Take walks

May you live all the days of your life.

Jonathan Swift

*Determine never to be idle…It is wonderful how
much may be done if we are always doing.*

Thomas Jefferson

Using this book

THIS SMALL BOOK CAN BE a mighty talisman. I hope it will remind you that a fuller, richer, happier life awaits... it just takes five minutes.

It is so important to keep *The Five-Minute Renaissance* nearby. Its very presence is a powerful reminder. Perhaps you come home from work, take care of some household business, fix dinner, eat, clean up, look at the mail, and yikes, it is nine o'clock and you are exhausted. You see *The Five-Minute Renaissance* on your nightstand. Five minutes, just five minutes. You do your activity. You feel great.

Maybe though, there is a better time. Throw the book into your bag and tomorrow you will see its cover and five minutes will pop up. Possibly there are five free minutes at lunchtime, or right before you leave work. Who knows? But the physical presence of *The Five-Minute Renaissance* will constantly remind you that, yes, you do have five minutes and you can do the thing that you really want to do.

Acknowledgements

I AM DEEPLY GRATEFUL TO so many people who helped me along the way. I wish to thank friends and family, especially Jennifer, Diane, Geoffrey, Bill, Roger, Kate, and Susan for their love, encouragement and support. I am indebted to Jan Jalenak, Nick Abrams, Susan Shacter, Noah Press and Tom Slaughter for their brilliance.

A special thank you to Imogene and Ella who were and continue to be my inspiration.

Breinigsville, PA USA
01 March 2010
233311BV00005B/1/P